CONTENTS

THE RIGHT TO BE WHO YOU ARE

The letters LGBTQ+ stand for the words: Lesbian, Gay, Bisexual, Transgender and Queer or Questioning. LGBTQ describes people who love others of the same sex as them; people who love both sexes; men who identify as women and women who identify as men; and those who are exploring how they feel.

The + represents some of the other ways that people live their lives and love each other.

These identities are placed together because the people who identify with them face similar issues or prejudices. They often join together to help each other fight for equal rights.

For hundreds of years, LGBTQ+ people have struggled to be accepted. They have been turned away from jobs, refused homes or denied healthcare. Many have been bullied, attacked or even killed because of who they love, how they dress or because some people see them as 'different'.

LGBTQ+ people have the right to be treated the same as everyone else and the right to be protected from harm. Rights are the basic freedoms that everyone deserves. Rights should protect everyone no matter who they are or where they live.

LGBTQ+ IN THE PAST

Some LGBTQ+ people had different rights in the past. For example, at times in ancient Egypt it didn't matter if you had a same-sex relationship. In fact, gay marriages were a cause for big celebrations for many ancient Egyptians. And many Egyptian gods were partly male and partly female or something different to either male or female.

Other LGBTQ+ people in the past were treated badly. Being gay was sometimes treated as an illness that doctors tried to cure. LGBTQ+ people were often forced to hide their feelings and relationships.

If they didn't hide, they could be attacked or sent away from their homes and communities. There were even laws against being LGBTQ+. From the 13th to the 18th centuries in France, people who were gay could be punished by being killed.

LGBTQ+ RIGHTS

Many LGBTQ+ people around the world suffered unfairness and violence for hundreds of years. Gradually, things began to change. In the late 19th and early 20th centuries, some people were inspired to fight for LGBTQ+ rights.

German doctor Magnus Hirschfeld was one such person. He risked his life and his reputation for others.

Hirschfeld was horrified when one of his patients took his own life because he couldn't live freely as a gay man. So, Hirschfield set about proving that people did not choose to be LGBTQ+, but were born that way. He hoped this would help people understand LGBTQ+ lives.

He started the world's first known LGBTQ+ rights group in Berlin, Germany in 1897. It was called the Scientific Humanitarian Committee.

Dr Hirschfield was insulted and regularly beaten for his views, but he did not stop. His LGBTQ+ rights group fought bravely to change laws that made being gay a crime. They fought for people to accept homosexuality.

TAKING A STAND

In spite of some progress, 50 years ago many LGBTQ+ people were still being attacked across the world. One dramatic night in 1969, things started to change.

On 28 June that year, police stormed into the Stonewall Inn bar in New York City, USA. The police regularly did these raids to arrest the LGBTQ+ people who met there. On this night, one member of the LGBTQ+ community, Marsha P. Johnson, refused to leave quietly with the police.

The police started to beat people and a fight broke out. Others came to join the struggle and protesters were still chanting "*Gay power!*" outside the bar a week later.

The Stonewall uprising in New York City became famous. It encouraged many more LGBTQ+ people to take a stand. Within a year, the Gay Liberation Front and other groups were set up around the world to fight for LGBTQ+ rights.

MARCHING WITH PRIDE

On the first anniversary of the Stonewall uprising, on 28 June 1970, there was a huge march in New York City. Over 2,000 LGBTQ+ people took to the streets to show the world that they were not ashamed of who they were. Together they chanted "*Say it loud, gay is proud*".

This Pride march was the first of many. Pride marches soon became an annual event and today they happen in countries all over the world. These joyous, colourful events celebrate LGBTQ+ people and the fight for their equality.

SAY IT LOUD, GAY IS PROUD!

In 1978 American artist Gilbert Baker designed and made a new flag to be carried during a march in a city in California. The rainbow colours of the flag represent the range of different people in the LGBTQ+ community. This rainbow flag soon became a symbol for gay pride and LGBTQ+ people around the world. It is now used during Pride events everywhere.

MARCHING WITH PRIDE!

We're QUEER and we're HERE!

LGBTQ+ LEADERS

The idea for a Pride flag came from Harvey Milk. In 1977 Milk became the first openly gay man to be elected as an official for a US state government.

Milk worked hard to improve life for everyone in San Francisco, California and to win more rights for LGBTQ+ people. For example, he stopped a plan to sack gay teachers.

But Milk faced hatred and daily death threats for his efforts. Sadly he was shot dead in 1978, less than a year after people voted him into his job.

A big breakthrough for LGBTQ+ rights came more than 30 years later. In 2009 an Icelandic politician, Jóhanna Sigurðardóttir, became the prime minister of Iceland. She was the first openly lesbian and LGBTQ+ person to lead a government in modern history.

Like Milk and other LGBTQ+ politicians, Sigurðardóttir worked for everyone in her country. She said that during her time as leader, she tried to make all of her decisions with equality in mind.

LGBTQ+ AND THE ARMED FORCES

People have to fight for LGBTQ+ rights in all walks of life. Throughout history many countries banned LGBTQ+ people from joining the army, navy or air force. Those who did join the armed forces often faced bullying, ill-treatment and violence if found out. The fight for equal rights is changing this.

In 1976, Sweden became one of the first countries in the world to officially allow LGBTQ+ people to join the military. For the Swedish armed forces, it was not just a question of equality, they also see people's differences as a strength.

Leaders of the Swedish armed forces march in Pride parades and encourage LGBTQ+ people to join the military. In 2018, they made an advert showing soldiers with the rainbow Pride flag across their faces. The caption said:

"We don't always march straight. No matter when or where we march, we always stand up for your right to live the way you want with whoever you want."
(Swedish Armed Forces, 2018)

LGBTQ+ IN SPORT

In the past, LGBTQ+ people were often left out of sports teams and tournaments because of prejudice. It was also because of stereotypes: unfair ideas, such as gay men being no good at football. LGBTQ+ athletes winning medals and breaking records made a big difference.

Martina Navratilova is a world famous tennis champion from the Czech Republic. She was one of the world's first athletes to say she was homosexual.

She faced prejudice and stereotyping all through her career. She missed out on a lot of sponsorship money because companies did not want to be linked to a lesbian. Her success and fight for equal rights gave a lot of other LGBTQ+ sports people the courage to play.

In the 2018 Winter Olympics, more athletes were open about being LGBTQ+ than ever before. Eric Radford from Canada became the first openly gay champion at the Winter Olympics when he won a gold medal for ice skating.

The success of these athletes inspires other LGBTQ+ people to follow their sporting dreams.

HIV, AIDS AND PREJUDICE

In the 1980s, doctors in San Francisco, California, USA noticed that healthy gay men were dying from the condition that became known as AIDS – a disease caused by a virus called HIV. At that time AIDS was a new disease and no one knew how to stop it or cure it. News reports scared people about how dangerous AIDS could be.

Rumours started about how AIDS was spread, which made some people wrongly blame LGBTQ+ people – especially gay men – for the disease. Instead of being helped, gay people were often avoided, forced out of communities and jobs, and even attacked.

The LGBTQ+ community pulled together to protest against the scaremongering and hate. They joined marches and organisations. They demanded their right to decent healthcare, more information about how to stay safe and they called for governments to spend more money to help in the crisis.

In 1987, an enormous, colourful quilt was displayed in the US capital, in Washington, D. C. Each of its 48,000 panels were made by different people to remember the LGBTQ+ loved ones they had lost to AIDS. This became the world's largest community art project. It helped people to understand the tragic impact of AIDS.

SAME-SEX PARTNERS

Some same-sex couples choose to live together without being married. Others want to show their love for each other by taking marriage vows. They have fought against laws that stop same-sex couples from marrying.

At first, some countries started to offer same-sex couples a civil partnership as an alternative to marriage. This gives same-sex couples similar rights and responsibilities as a married couple. Denmark was the first country to have civil partnerships in 1989.

Marriage ceremonies are different. They usually take place in front of a religious leader and some religious people believe marriage must only be between a man and a woman. This started to change in 2001 when the Netherlands became the first country in the world to allow same-sex marriage. That day, the Mayor of Amsterdam married four same-sex couples.

Today, same sex marriage is possible in over 30 countries around the world.

PEACEFUL PROTESTS

People have tried many different ways to protest for LGBTQ+ rights and to bring LGBTQ+ issues to the world's attention.

In 2019, students at a high school in Taiwan organised a week-long event encouraging male students and teachers to wear skirts. Their idea was to break down gender stereotypes. The event was such a success that the school has dropped gender-specific uniforms. Now both male and female students are allowed to wear skirts.

Katlego Kolanyane-Kesupile fights for LGBTQ+ rights with poetry and plays. In 2013, she was the first transgender person to come out openly in Botswana.

People are known as transgender if they were born a female, but feel that they are really a man, or born male and feel that they are a woman. Katlego Kolanyane-Kesupile was insulted and attacked for being transgender. So, she set up the Queer Shorts Showcase Festival in 2014. The festival shows plays about LGBTQ+ lives and tackles some of the lies that are told about LGBTQ+ people.

Changing people's ideas about LGBTQ+ lives can make a real difference. In 2019, lesbian and gay people were given the right to live openly in Botswana. It is hoped that these rights will spread to all parts of Africa.

TRANSGENDER RIGHTS

Everyone should have the right to be themselves, but in the past transgender people were told there was something wrong with them.

It took a long time to prove that being transgender is an essential part of who someone is. In 2018, the World Health Organization said that being transgender should no longer be defined as a mental illness.

LBGTQ+ people have been fighting for the right to decide who they are for themselves. In some countries, transgender people can only change their identity on important documents, such as passports, if a doctor approves.

In 2014, Denmark became the first country in Europe to allow transgender adults to choose their own identity on documents.

On Danish passports, there are boxes for male, female or 'X'. The X represents people who identify as male, female, male and female, or as neither.

LGBTQ+ RIGHTS TODAY

Around the world people have braved insults, challenges and threats to improve the rights of LGBTQ+ people. Their efforts have made a huge difference. Today more LGBTQ+ people than ever before live freely and in safety. However, the fight for equal rights is far from over.

In too many countries, being LGBTQ+ still means being denied a job, living with discrimination, name-calling and bullying, or even violence. It is still a crime to be lesbian or gay in around 70 countries and in some of these, LGBTQ+ people can still be punished by death.

In July 2013, the United Nations launched the Free & Equal campaign. It called for equal rights and fair treatment of LGBTQ+ people. The campaign tells the world that the fight for LGBTQ+ rights is very important.

We can all get involved by learning more, talking about and standing up for the rights of LGBTQ+ people everywhere.

LGBTQ+ TIMELINE

Here is a list of moments in history covered in this book that help to tell the story of the fight for LGBTQ+ rights.

500 BCE: Gay marriages are celebrated in certain times and parts of ancient Egypt. Many Egyptian gods were partly male and partly female or something different to either male or female.

1200–1700: In France, people who are gay are punished by being killed or thrown out of their communities.

1897: Magnus Hirschfield starts the world's first known LGBTQ+ rights group in Berlin, Germany. It is called the Scientific Humanitarian Committee.

1969: The Stonewall uprising in New York City, USA is sparked by police entering the Stonewall Inn.

1970: The first Pride march takes place in New York City, USA.

1976: Sweden becomes one of the first countries in the world to allow LGBTQ+ people to join the military.

1977: Harvey Milk becomes the first openly gay man to be elected as an official of member of a US state government. He is shot dead in 1978.

1978: American artist Gilbert Baker designs and makes a new rainbow flag to be carried at Pride marches.

1980s: Doctors discover a new disease called AIDS. Gay men in particular are (wrongly) blamed for the spread of the disease and many are attacked.

1980s: Martina Navratilova becomes the first openly gay tennis champion.

1987: The AIDS Memorial Quilt is displayed for the first time on the National Mall in Washington, D.C.

1989: Denmark is the first country to allow civil partnerships.

2001: The Netherlands becomes the first country in the world to allow same-sex marriages.

2009: Jóhanna Sigurðardóttir becomes the prime minister of Iceland and the first openly LGBTQ+ person to lead a government in modern history.

2013: The United Nations launches the Free & Equal campaign. It calls for equal rights and fair treatment of all LGBTQ+ people.

2014: Denmark becomes the first country in Europe to allow transgender adults to choose their own identity on documents.

2018: Canadian ice skater, Eric Radford becomes the first openly gay Winter Olympic champion.

2018: The World Health Organization declares that being transgender should no longer be defined as a mental illness.

GLOSSARY

AIDS an illness caused by the HIV virus, which weakens a person's immune system, making them more likely to suffer from serious infections or diseases

ancient Egypt an ancient civilisation that existed around 5,000–2,000 years ago in lands that are now in modern Egypt

bisexual person who is attracted to both men and women

come out when someone tells other people they are gay, bi, trans or other

discrimination when people are treated unfairly because of things such as their gender or appearance

gay attracted to people of the same sex, used especially of a man, but also used by some women

gender a person's gender can be different to their sex. For example, they may have a boy's body parts, but feel more like a girl

gender identity the gender a person feels most comfortable as

homosexuality being attracted to people of the same sex

lesbian a woman who is attracted to other women

openly without hiding something

prejudice when someone dislikes anyone from a particular group of people, without even knowing them

queer originally used as a hate term, some people want to reclaim the word; to do with sexual or gender identity

questioning a person who is still exploring their sexuality or their gender identity

sex a person's sex describes whether they were born with male or female body parts

stereotype an idea or belief about someone you don't know based on things like their gender or appearance

transgender someone who was born female, but feels that they are really a man, or was born a male but feels that they are really a woman

United Nations an organisation set up to help solve world problems and that represents the people of 193 countries of the world

World Health Organization an organisation that is part of the United Nations. It was set up to look after the health and well-being of people around the world

BOOKS TO READ

Children in Our World: Rights and Equality by Marie Murray and illustrated by Hanane Kai (Wayland, 2021)

I'm a Global Citizen: Human Rights by Alice Harman and illustrated by David Broadbent (Franklin Watts, 2020)

My Life, Your Life: Understanding Sexuality by Honor Head (Franklin Watts, 2019)

My Life, Your Life: Understanding Transgender by Honor Head (Franklin Watts, 2019)

INDEX

Franklin Watts
First published in Great Britain in 2021 by The Watts Publishing Group
Copyright © The Watts Publishing Group, 2021

All rights reserved.

HB ISBN: 978 1 4451 7136 4
PB ISBN: 978 1 4451 7138 8

Printed and bound in Dubai

Editor: Amy Pimperton
Designer: Peter Scoulding
Cover design: Peter Scoulding
Illustrations: Toby Newsome

Page 2 photograph
© Amy Lamé

Franklin Watts, an imprint of
Hachette Children's Group
Carmelite House
50 Victoria Embankment
London EC4Y 0DZ

An Hachette UK Company
www.hachette.co.uk
www.franklinwatts.co.uk

All facts and statistics were correct
at the time of printing.

FSC
www.fsc.org
MIX
Paper from
responsible sources
FSC® C104740